managing
PROJECTS

MANAGEMENT SERIES FROM NEW DAWN PRESS

Managing Leadership

Managing People

Managing Sales

Managing Time

Managing Stress

Managing Projects

Managing Text Messaging

managing PROJECTS

S K Palhan

Sterling Paperbacks

STERLING PAPERBACKS
An imprint of
Sterling Publishers (P) Ltd.
A-59, Okhla Industrial Area, Phase-II,
New Delhi-110020.
Tel: 26387070, 26386209; Fax: 91-11-26383788
E-mail: mail@sterlingpublishers.com
www.sterlingpublishers.com

Managing Projects
Copyright © 2005, Sterling Publishers Pvt. Ltd.
ISBN 978 81 207 5677 9
Reprint 2009, 2010

All rights are reserved.
No part of this publication may be reproduced, stored in a retrieval system or transmitted, in any form or by any means, mechanical, photocopying, recording or otherwise, without prior written permission of the original publisher.

Printed in India
Printed and Published by Sterling Publishers Pvt. Ltd.,
New Delhi-110 020.

Contents

Project Management — 7
    What is a project?
    Managing a project
    Stages of a project
Project Conceptualisation and Definition — 11
    Sources of a project
    Definition of a project
        Statement of requirements
        List of stakeholders
        Project brief
        Scope of work statement (SOW)
        Risk assessment
Project Planning — 22
    Identifying key stages
    Preparing a project logic diagram
    Formatting the work breakdown structure (WBS)

    Allocating responsibilities for key stages
    Estimating duration
    Formulating PERT and critical path
    Scheduling activities
    Analysing resource requirement
    Project budgeting and approval
Project Implementation   59
    Project launching
    Organisational structure
    Effective communication
    Management of project problems
    Project logbook
    Project monitoring
    Application of computers
Project Handover Phase   82
    Concluding Tasks
    Termination Procedure
Glossary   87

Project Management

What is a project?

A project is a collection of linked activities, carried out in an organised manner, with a clearly defined start and end point. The objective of a project is to achieve specific results in order to satisfy the strategic needs of the organisation. Project work is beyond the routine business activities of an organisation. The activities in the project have a precedence relationship, i.e. certain activities must be completed before a new activity can be started on account of administrative or technological considerations.

Some typical examples of a project are as follows:

- Construction of a 500 MW thermal power station
- Construction of an underground railway
- Construction of a bridge across a river
- Setting up of a restaurant or a factory
- Publication of a book/newsletter

Managing a project

Project management is a dynamic process which utilises appropriate resources of the organisation in a controlled and structured manner to achieve some clearly-defined objectives which have been identified as strategic needs. Projects have to be managed within a defined set of constraints in terms of time, cost or manpower available. Completion of the project within the stipulated time is extremely important because delays in the project would lead to the following problems:

- Increase in the cost of the project through
  - wage bill
  - interest on investment made in the project
- Customer dissatisfaction
- Loss of revenue if the project is for revenue generation (e.g. a power station or a petrol pump)

Hence, timely execution of the project is one of the most important objectives of project management. The purpose of planning is also to ensure that all the activities are identified and scheduled to complete the project in time. Project management includes classical functions like planning, organisation, coordination and control.

A project involves teamwork and problem solving at various stages.

Stages of a project

A project goes through four fundamental stages:

Project conception and definition: It defines the needs of the project in agreement with those people who have an interest in the outcome of the project.

Project planning: This involves the process of planning the project to devise a realistic schedule, taking into account the constraints imposed on the project.

Project execution: It includes launching the project and ensuring that everyone in the team understands clearly the activities as well as the constraints. The activities are carried out taking into account any changes which may occur in the plan.

Project closing and handover to the customer: This includes preparing the customer for acceptance and handover, ensuring that the project has delivered the agreed results, and the project evaluation process.

These four stages are merely convenient categories devised to understand the project. In reality, most projects would have a significant amount of reiteration. At any stage of project implementation, there may be revision in the project definition, replan of the work and also rescheduling of activities. The dynamics of the project ensures that the right things are done to get the desired results.

Project Conceptualisation and Definition

Project conceptualisation and definition refers to the development of the vision of the project and establishment of the goals set by it. For this purpose, the first activity is the collection of relevant data. The definition of the project is the process of putting together the data in a systematic order. A clear definition of the project is very important for its success. A large number of projects fail because they have poor or unclear definition. Besides, projects often face a number of conflicts that have to be resolved.

The goals of a project have to be clearly defined to specify what is hoped to be achieved on the completion of the project. The outcomes of the project, in terms of deliverables and the benefit to the stakeholders and end users, should be well-defined. The success of the project will be judged on the basis of the goals identified. The goals are usually set up by the people responsible for the approval of a project. The project goals are refined or focused by the project leader in consultation with key stakeholders.

Sources of a project

A project may be conceived for the following reasons:

- To meet the corporate objectives (e.g. the company wants to add a manufacturing facility to its trading business)
- To introduce step changes in an organisation (e.g. introduction of ISO-9001 certification of facilities)
- To fulfil a need or capitalise on opportunities (e.g. to set up an export house or a service centre at a new location)
- To comply with revised norms or legislations (e.g. to develop a new engine to meet the revised pollution norms decided by the government)

In the case of some organisations, their regular activities may be in the nature of projects (e.g. devising of programs by software development companies, construction of houses and bridges, setting up of power stations or publishing of books).

Projects which involve a step change are directly derived from the organisation's vision. It is important to understand the context in which a project is proposed to meet the future needs of the organisation.

In the initial stage, a project is usually hazy and ill-defined. The purpose of the conceptualisation of a project is to define it in consultation with the people who have an interest in the outcome of the project.

Definition of a project

A project is essentially defined through the following documents:
- Statement of requirements
- List of stakeholders
- Project brief
- Scope of work statement (SOW)
- Risk assessment

For defining a project, the following documents have to be prepared:

Statement of requirements: This refers to what is required (deliverables) at the end of the project. This is important since the customer or the sponsor of the project may also not be very clear about the deliverables. The expectations of the client tend to increase as the project makes progress. The written approval of the customer is desirable to maintain commitment to the project. This does not mean that no changes or suggestions of the customer would be entertained; in fact, changes do take place in practice and the project team has to handle them appropriately if the expectations of the customer involve increased cost and time for completion.

List of stakeholders: It is important to list the people who have an interest in the outcome of the project (the interest may be now or at a later stage of the project). These include the following:

- Customers
- End users
- Project sponsors
- Members of the project team
- The finance/purchase department
- Suppliers/contractors
- Consultants
- The public (positively or negatively affected by the project)
- Concerned regulatory bodies (e.g. the environmental board)

The fact that the stakeholders have an interest in the project implies that they may have an agenda of their own for the project. Stakeholders can be an asset in project management but, if not handled properly, they can become major obstacles in the progress of the project.

For example, in the construction of a river valley dam project, the people who have to be evacuated and rehabilitated suitably, may become a hindrance to the project if they are not handled properly by the project management team.

The project stakeholders have to be kept informed about the progress of the project and also consulted at appropriate times. Therefore a list of stakeholders should be kept ready always. This list should include the following items of information:

- Name
- Address
- Telephone number
- Status (internal and external)

The key interest of each stakeholder in the project should also be noted in this list. A format for this is given in Figure 1.

Figure 1: Project stakeholders' list

Project stakeholders' list							
Title of Project:								
Date :						Project Manager:		
Line No.	Stakeholder	Name	Location	Tel No.	Internal	External	Monitoring person
1.							
2.							
3.							
4.							
5.							
6.							
7.							
8.							

Project brief: The project brief contains the overall information about the project compiled after consultation with the team members and the stakeholders. The project file usually starts with a project brief. It should contain the following information on a single page:

- Project title – this is given to identify the project, e.g. 'Publication of Book ABC'
- Project overall objective – this indicates the desired results of the project in a few lines
- Project leader and project sponsor

- Project proposed start date – this refers to the date when the project definition would be approved for starting
- Project duration and termination date
- Project deliverables – these are the identifiable outputs of the project. The project deliverables should be SMART, i.e.
    - S - Specific
    - M - Measurable
    - A - Achievable
    - R - Realistic
    - T - Time-bound
- Project benefits – these identify the benefits to the customer/organisation in quantitative terms, e.g. cost savings, profitability, etc.
- Project strategy – this identifies a specific route which is proposed to achieve the objective, e.g. whether a road would be built using cement or bitumen
- Project skills required – this identifies the major technical skills which are required in the project, e.g. designing, construction, computer software, etc.
- Relation with other projects – this becomes important when the project under implementation is a part of a major project,

e.g. a pump house may be part of a large agricultural farm project
- Project cost – it indicates the total cost of the project. It is usually an estimate in the beginning and it is subject to revisions and becomes more realistic after the planning is completed
- Risk management – this identifies the risks which are likely to arise in the project

Scope of work statement (SOW): This includes the objectives in greater detail. It also limits the boundary of the project (i.e. what is not included in the project). The deliverables are identified in more specific terms. Scope of work also includes the constraints and assumptions under which the project is to be implemented.

Some typical items included in the SOW are as follows:
- Product specifications decided by the customer
- Mandatory standards to be complied with
- Process specifications
- Standard operating procedures
- Purchasing procedures
- Subcontracting terms and conditions to be imposed on suppliers
- Quality standards applicable

The SOW also indicates the reference from which detailed information is available regarding specifications, standards, etc.

Risk assessment: For successful project management, risks should be identified beforehand. Bad weather, strikes by employees, accidents and delay in supplies are some of the risks. A risk is any event that could prevent the realisation of the project, thereby affecting the expectations of the stakeholders. A risk that becomes a reality is termed as an 'issue'.

Project risks are of two types:
- Project risks due to the technical nature of work in the project
- Process risks associated with processes, procedures, equipment, technology, controls, communication and team performance

It is the project manager's job to discuss the following points with the team:
- Identify and evaluate potential risks
- Obtain agreement on action plans to contain the risks
- Take suitable action and monitor the results
- Promptly resolve the issues when the risk becomes a reality

Risks identified may not be equally likely and their impact on the project schedule and cost may also be different. Therefore it becomes important to rank the risks as follows:

- The risk may be ranked according to the probability of its happening, i.e. becoming an issue. The probability of occurrence may be ranked on a scale of 1 to 9. Rating 1 means low probability and Rating 9 means high probability, i.e. likely to become an issue.
- The risk may be ranked on the basis of its impact on the schedule and the project cost.

The probability and the impact of a risk may be analysed in the risk ranking matrix given in Figure 2.

Figure 2: Risk ranking matrix

		Impact on the project		
		LOW	MEDIUM	HIGH
PROBABILITY	7-9	Medium	High	Not acceptable
	4-6	Low	High	Not acceptable
	1-3	Low	Medium	High

The identified risks are ranked as high, medium and low, as shown in the table. The high ranked risks have a major impact on the project schedule and cost and therefore must be monitored regularly. In the core project team, responsibility should be allocated to different members to monitor the risks which are ranked high and medium. They are listed in the project risk log.

Project Planning

In project planning, all the activities of the project such as goals, resources to be committed, estimation of time and prioritisation of various activities have to be clearly stated. Areas of responsibility must be identified and assigned. The time schedule and resources have to be forecast and budgeted.

The project schedule identifies the sequence of activities including the starting and scheduled completion date.

The project core team has to be formed before project planning starts. The core team should have the required skills. The project plan helps to guide the work from start to finish. It identifies the work to be done and it is also a tool for communicating with the stakeholders and the members of the project team.

The major components of a project plan are as follows:
- Identifying key stages
- Preparing a project logic diagram
- Formatting the work breakdown structure (WBS)
- Allocating responsibilities for key stages
- Estimating duration
- Formulating PERT and critical path
- Scheduling activities
- Analysing resource requirement
- Project budgeting and approval

Identifying key stages

The first step in the planning process is to identify the work as a list of tasks to complete the project. The list of tasks is identified by the collective experience of the team through the process of 'brain storming'.

- All the members of the team should understand clearly the objectives and scope of the project.
- Each member is asked to identify the tasks and the same are recorded on a board.

- The suggestions are not subjected to any discussion or value judgement, i.e. critical comments are not allowed.
- In the subsequent rounds, members can elaborate on the list of tasks.

The list of tasks identified thus is not ranked with any priorities at this stage. The duplicate tasks, if any, are removed and then the rest are clustered to gather those tasks that are clearly related. For example, issuing a tender notice, analysing the offers received and placing an order for an item may be clubbed together. Such activities may be done in series or parallelly. The task list should be reduced to a reasonable number of activities, preferably in the range of 30 to 60, depending on the size of the project. These activities are the key stages of a project. Some tasks may be later added to the key stages to complete them.

At this stage the following precautions should be taken:

- Time estimation and scheduling should be avoided
- Assigning persons to key stages should not be done

Preparing a project logic diagram

In order to be able to monitor the progress of a project at a glance, a project logic diagram should be made with fixed milestones.

Milestones are not tasks, but represent the completion of the work that has been performed till a particular point on the project logic diagram. The key stages have to be arranged in a logical order according to the sequence in which the tasks have to be completed. The purposes of a project logic diagram are as follows:

- To show the sequence of relationship among the tasks to complete a project i.e. which activity must be completed before starting off with the others
- To identify the milestones in the project in order to monitor its progress
- To show the relationship of a specific task to different parts of the task list and the work breakdown structure (WBS)
- To show logically at a glance how the project will be completed

The key stages are written separately on notelets of a sticker pad. The first key stage is labelled **Start** and the last stage is labelled **Finish**. All the key stages are arranged on a sheet, board or wall. The **Start** stage is the first one on the left-hand side. All the notelets are fixed at appropriate places, taking the precedence logic into account. The notelets are connected by an arrow (→) to show the logical flow of the project from **Start** to **Finish**.

The whole project team should be involved in developing the project logic diagram. The basic premise of the project logic diagram is that a new activity cannot logically start until all the immediate previous activities finish. The project logic diagram is used extensively for scheduling activities as well as for monitoring the progress of the project.

The project logic diagram may be prepared using the checklist given below.

- Prepare a separate notelet for each key stage.
- Place a **Start** notelet at the extreme left of the sheet.
- Place a **Finish** notelet at the extreme right of the sheet.
- Do not prepare a time scale on the diagram.
- Start each key stage description with a verb (in the present tense).
- Do not attempt to add durations for the key stages yet.

- Locate the notelets on the sheet in order of dependency (debate each location if required).
- When all the notelets are used up, check the dependencies (by working backwards, i.e. from **Finish** to **Start**).
- Show the dependency links as **Finish** to **Start** relationships initially.
- Do not take people doing the work into account – this can produce errors.
- Do not add in responsibilities at this stage.
- Draw in the dependency links with straight arrows in pencil.
- Avoid arrows crossing, as they lead to confusion.
- Label each key stage with an alphanumeric code: A-1, B-2, C-3, etc.
- When satisfied that the diagram is correct, record the dependencies in the table as shown.
- If appropriate, tape the notelets down to the sheet, then roll it up for filing.

An example of a project logic diagram is given in Figure 4. The key stages of setting up a hospital project have been identified in Figure 3 and the project logic diagram has been drawn up based on these stages.

Figure 3: Key stages in a hospital project

Activity	Description	Immediate Predecessor(s)
A-1	Select doctors	–
B-2	Survey and select site	–
C-3	Select equipment and furniture	A-1
D-4	Prepare final construction plans and layout	B-2
E-5	Bring utilities to site	B-2
F-6	Interview applicants and select staff for nursing, administrative support, maintenance and security	A-1
G-7	Purchase and take delivery of equipment	C-3
H-8	Construct hospital	D-4
I-9	Develop information system	A-1
J-10	Install equipment and furniture	E-5, G-7, H-8, I-9
K-11	Train nurses and support staff	F-6, J-10

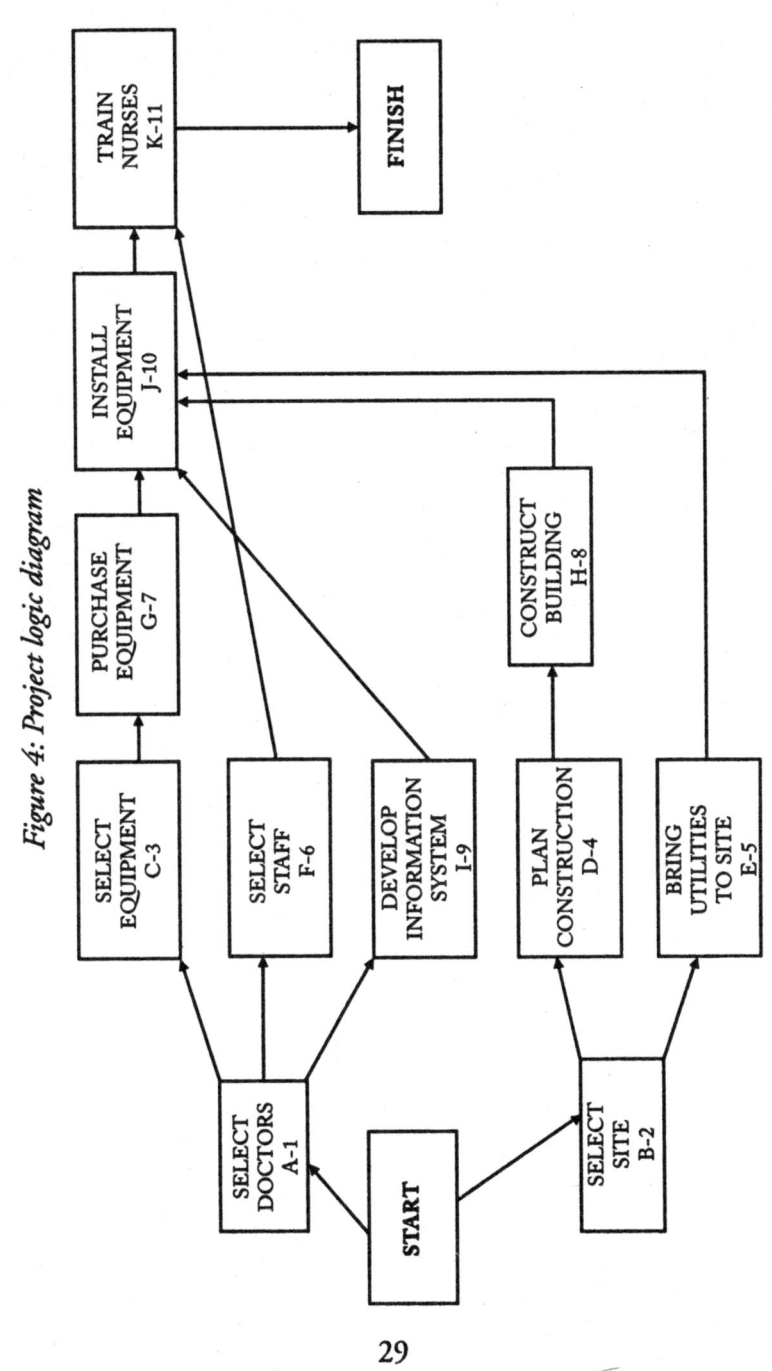

Figure 4: Project logic diagram

Formatting the work breakdown structure (WBS)

The work breakdown structure (WBS) is a basic diagram that describes the hierarchy of all the work that must be done to complete the project. The WBS forms the basis for the networking diagram, scheduling, costing and work assignment. The WBS breaks the total project into smaller packages of work called tasks. The WBS has certain definite advantages.

- The work is broken into a logical sequence of tasks for completion. It shows how the different tasks fit into the project and how one task may overlap or interfere with another task if not finished on time.
- The WBS divides the tasks into different modules which are manageable.
- The WBS helps to identify the different skills which would be required to complete the project.
- It helps to determine the number of people required.
- It helps in communication of the work to be done without going into too much detail.
- It helps in understanding the sequence of the work to be completed.

In the WBS three terms are important.

- *Milestone* marks the completion of an important set of tasks or an important event in the project (e.g. construction of the building in the hospital project).
- *Task* is a cohesive unit of work in a project. It is neither too small nor too big for tracking the progress of the project.
- *Subtask* (an element of work) is an activity required to complete a project, but it is too small to be treated as a task. For example, writing a letter, putting gum on the envelope, pasting the address slip, pasting a stamp, taking the envelope to the letter box and putting it into the letter box would be subtasks or elements of work.

The WBS of a project breaks the project work into key stages in the first level. In the second level, each key stage is broken into tasks and in the third level, each task may be broken into subtasks. A WBS may have three levels in a simple project but in a large project, each key stage may be a project by itself. Large projects may have more than ten levels.

In some cases, it may be inconvenient to draw a WBS on one page. In such cases we may use an outline-style WBS. An example of an outline WBS is given in Figure 5.

The WBS is a dynamic tool which must be updated as the work proceeds, because some of the tasks and elements may be changed during the implementation of the project.

Allocating responsibilities for key stages

Each key stage of a project needs to be owned by one of the team members. The allocation of responsibility is important to ensure timely completion of the work. Members of the project team may accept more than one key stage. The responsibility of a key stage owner is to confirm the following:

- The work required is identified at the task level
- The dependencies of tasks (i.e. procedures) are clearly defined
- The estimated duration of a task is accurate
- The work is done on time maintaining the required quality standard
- The work is monitored regularly
- Status reports are prepared accurately and issued on time

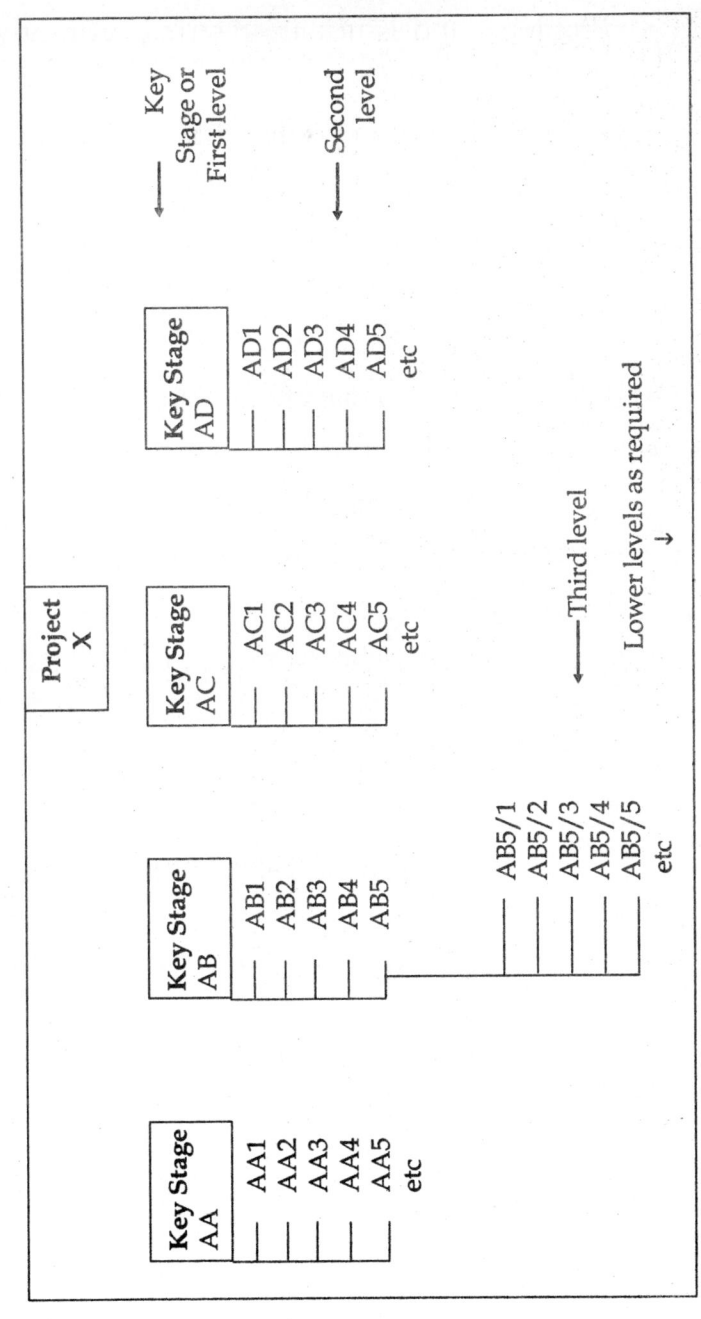

Figure 5: Outline WBS

- Problems and issues are referred promptly to the project manager

The ownership of key stages has to be allocated carefully, taking into account the following:

- Individual capability in terms of depth of knowledge, skill and previous experience
- Problem-solving ability
- Personal time management capability
- Current workload from other projects
- Ability to get along with others

To ensure efficiency, a linear responsibility chart (LRC) is drawn up to display key activities and the names of resources who have been allocated the responsibilities.

While allocating key stages/tasks, the project manager should also consider the availability of adequate tools, equipment and technical skills. The key stage responsibility chart is an important aspect of project planning and typical information recorded on it is as follows:

- Title of project
- Project sponsor
- Project manager
- Project customer

Each key stage has the following information in tabulated form:
- Description of the key stage
- Duration of the stage (in weeks or days)
- Owner of the key stage
- Planned end date (when derived)

Estimating duration

Timely completion of a project is very important and any delay adds to the cost of the project. Since each project is unique, standard time estimates may not be applicable. The duration of a stage depends on the size of the task (e.g. construction of a 1 km long road or 20 km long road) and also the number of persons involved in doing the task. A realistic estimation of time is important to meet the schedule agreed upon with the customer.

The estimate of the duration may be based on several sources.
- Past experience of similar work
- Expert opinion
- Historical data from other projects

The majority of people are not productive or engaged in project activities all the time. Sometimes,

20 per cent of the time available may be taken up by the following:
- Meetings (which are not a must for work), unforeseen events, search for information
- General interruptions in work due to equipment/electricity failure, unexpected visitors, communication failure, lack of infrastructure, personal conflicts, complexity of the project, mismanagement, etc.

In some cases there is wide variation in duration based on past experiences. For example, the time taken for approval of a proposal may be as brief as two days (most optimistic), but in most of the cases the approval may be received in five days. In such cases, the duration of an activity is estimated by the formula

$$t_e = \frac{t_o + 4 t_m + t_p}{6}$$

where t_e = estimated duration of time
  t_o = most optimistic time
  t_m = most likely time
  t_p = most pessimistic time

The major cause of increase in the cost of projects is increased duration. Therefore the accuracy of estimates is a key factor for the timely execution of projects.

There may be inaccuracy in time estimation due to unforeseen factors. Hence, contingencies should be added at suitable places.

For each key stage it is important to keep a record of the following:
- The estimate of time decided
- Any assumptions made during the estimation (e.g. number of persons and the type of technology used)
- The amount of contingencies which have been added at different places

Formulating PERT and critical path

PERT (Programme Evaluation Review Technique) is a technique that is used to follow the progress of a project and review its status at different stages.

The project logic diagram shows all the major activities of the project and their precedence relationships, i.e. which activities must be completed before the other dependent activities can be started (e.g. building a wall can start only after the foundation has been dug).

Making the diagram
Diagrammatically representing the project as a network requires the establishment of precedence

relationships between various activities. For complex projects, this task is essential because incorrect or omitted precedence relationships will result in costly delays. The precedence relationships are represented by a network diagram, consisting of nodes (circles or rectangles) and arcs (arrows) that depict the relationships between activities. Two different approaches may be used to create a network diagram. The first approach, the Activity-On-Arc (AOA) network, uses arcs to represent activities and nodes to represent events. An event is the point at which one or more activities are to be completed and one or more other activities are to begin. An event consumes neither time nor resources. Because the AOA approach emphasises activity connection points, we say that it is event-oriented. Here, the precedence relationships are such that an event cannot occur until all the preceding activities have been completed. A convention used in the AOA network is to number events sequentially from left to right (see Figure 8).

In the second approach, the Activity-On-Node (AON) network, the activities are represented on the node itself and the arrows only indicate the logical precedence requirement.

Figure 6: AOA and AON approaches to activity relationships

Activity On Arc AOA	Activity On Node AON	Activity Relationships
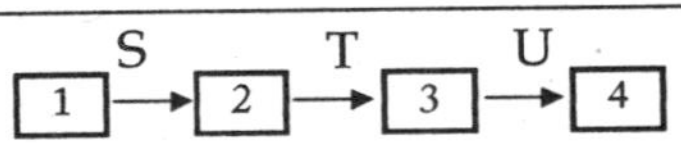 S→T→U (1→2→3→4)	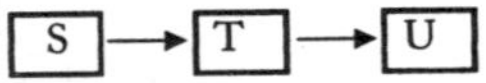 S→T→U	S precedes T, which precedes U.
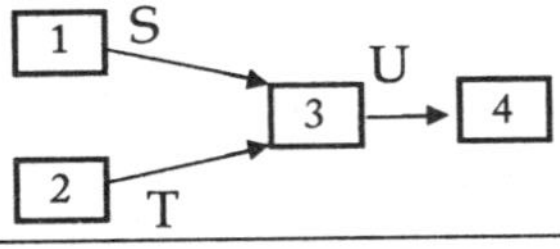 S, T → U (1→3, 2→3→4)	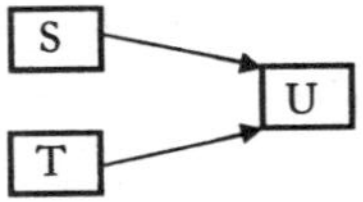 S, T → U	S and T must be completed before U can be started.
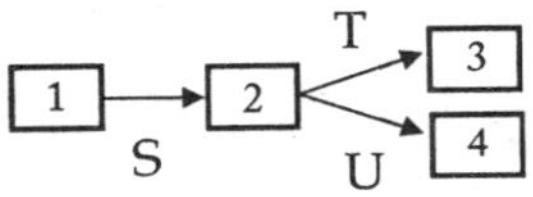 S → T, U (1→2→3, 2→4)	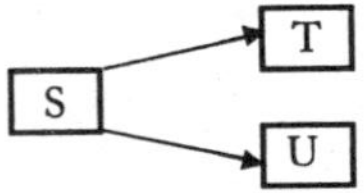 S → T, U	T and U cannot begin until S has been completed.
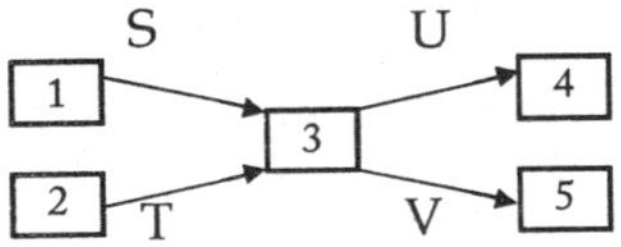 S, T → U, V (1→3, 2→3→4, 3→5)	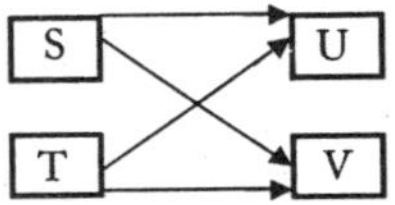 S, T → U, V	U and V cannot begin until both S and T have been completed.

39

Both the AON and the AOA approaches can accurately represent all the activities and precedence relationships in a project. However, the AOA approach often requires fewer nodes than the AON approach. Regardless of the approach used, modelling a large project as a network requires the manager to identify the necessary activities and recognise their precedence relationships. If this preplanning is skipped, a project often experiences unexpected delay.

In the following discussion of PERT and CPM (Critical Path Method), the AON convention will be used, although AOA diagrams can also be applied to all the procedures. The AON convention is used in most computerised project management systems.

A PERT node is usually represented as a rectangular box and each box contains the following information.

Earliest Start Time (EST)	Activity Duration	Earliest Finish Time (EST)
ACTIVITY DESCRIPTION		
Latest Start Time (LST)	Total Slack	Latest Finish Time (LFT)

PERT node

For understanding the practice of project management through PERT, let us study the example of a project for setting up a small hospital. The activities involved in such a project are given in Figure 7 (the predecessors for the activities have been also identified).

Figure 7: AON network for hospital project

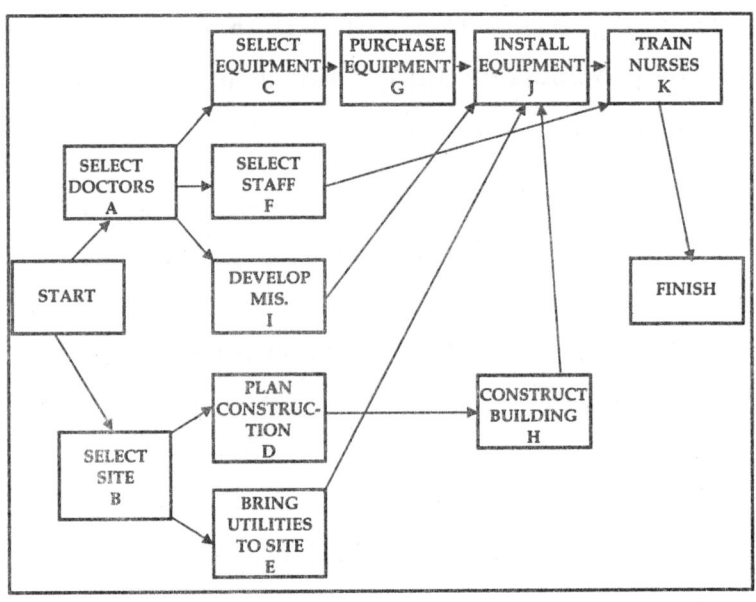

AON network

The AON network for the hospital project, based on their precedence relationships, is shown in Figure 7. It depicts activities in a chain, with arrows indicating the sequence in which they are to be performed. Activities A and B emanate from a start node because they have no immediate predecessors. The arrows connecting activity A to activities C, F and I indicate that all three require completion of activity A before they can begin. Similarly, activity B must be completed before activities D and E can begin, and so on. Activity K connects to a finish node because no activities follow it. The start and finish nodes do not actually represent activities, they merely provide beginning and ending points for the network.

AOA network

The AOA network is shown in Figure 8. Event 1 marks the beginning of the project. Activities A and B have no immediate predecessors; therefore the arrows representing those activities have event 1 as their base. Event 2 signals the completion of activity A. As activities C, F and I, all require the completion of A, the arrows representing these activities leave the node representing event 2. Similarly, the arrows for activities D and E leave the node for event 4, which signals the completion of activity B. The arrow for activity G leaves event 3, and event 6 is needed to tie activities G, H and E together, because they must be completed before activity J can begin.

For proper representation of the relationship for activity K, the use of a dummy activity is required.

Figure 8: AOA network for hospital project

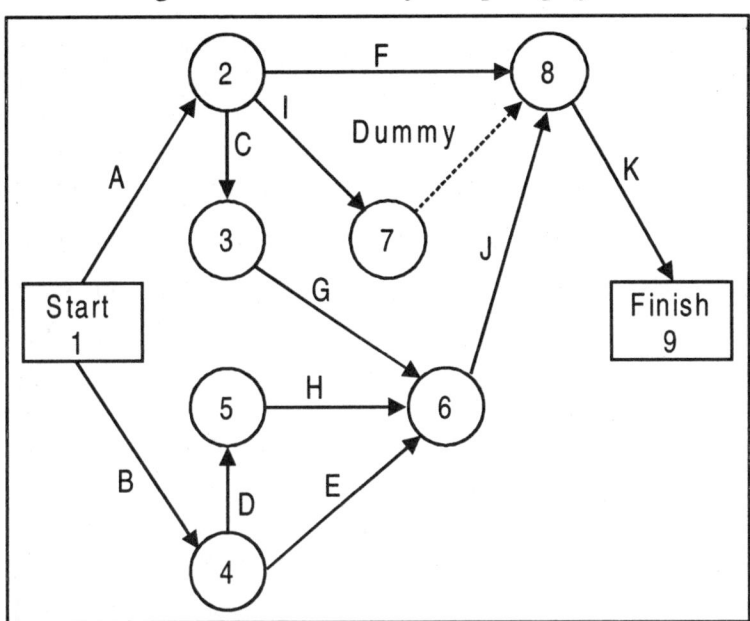

This dummy activity is represented by a dotted arrow. Activities I and F both emanate from event 2, and both must be completed before K can begin. Activities I and F will have the same beginning and ending nodes unless a dummy activity is used. Hence, event 7 signals the end of activity I, and event 8 signals the end of activity F, with a dummy activity joining them. Now all the activities are uniquely defined, and the network shows that activities F, I and J must be completed before activity K can begin. Event 9 indicates the completion of the project.

A crucial aspect of project management is estimating the time of completion. Figure 9 shows the estimated activity times calculated in weeks for completion of the hospital project. If each activity in setting up the hospital were done in sequence, with work proceeding on only one activity at a time, the time of completion would equal the sum of the times for all the activities, i.e. 175 weeks. However, the figure indicates that some of the activities can be carried on simultaneously.

Figure 9: Network for hospital project, showing activity times (in weeks)

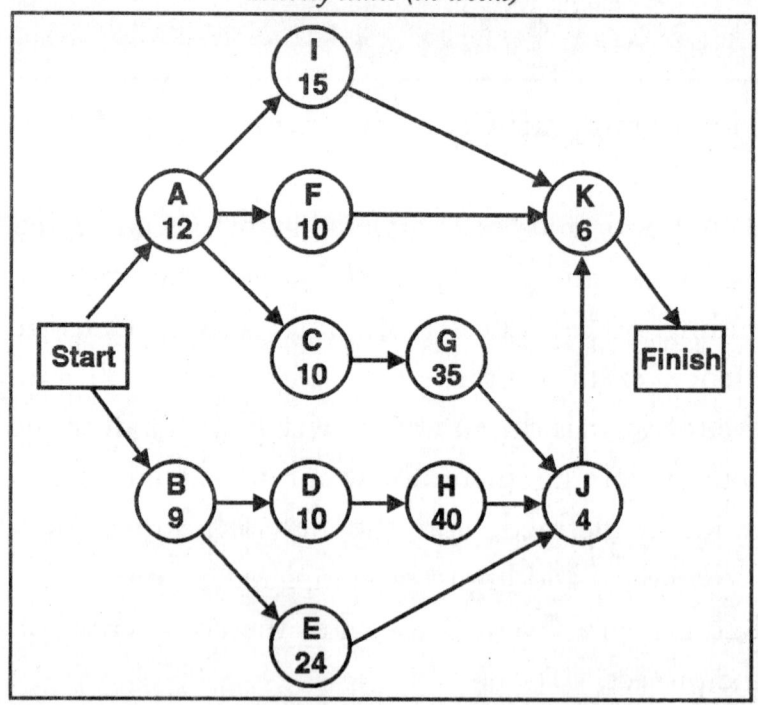

Each sequence of activities between the project's start and finish is called a path. Figure 10 shows that the network describing the hospital project has five paths: A-I-K, A-F-K, A-C-G-J-K, B-D-H-J-K and B-E-J-K. Of these, the critical path is the sequence of activities between a project's start and finish that takes the longest time to complete. Thus the activities along the critical path determine the completion time of the project; that is, if one of the activities on the critical path is delayed, the entire project will be delayed.

Figure 10: Activity paths for the hospital project, with the critical path highlighted

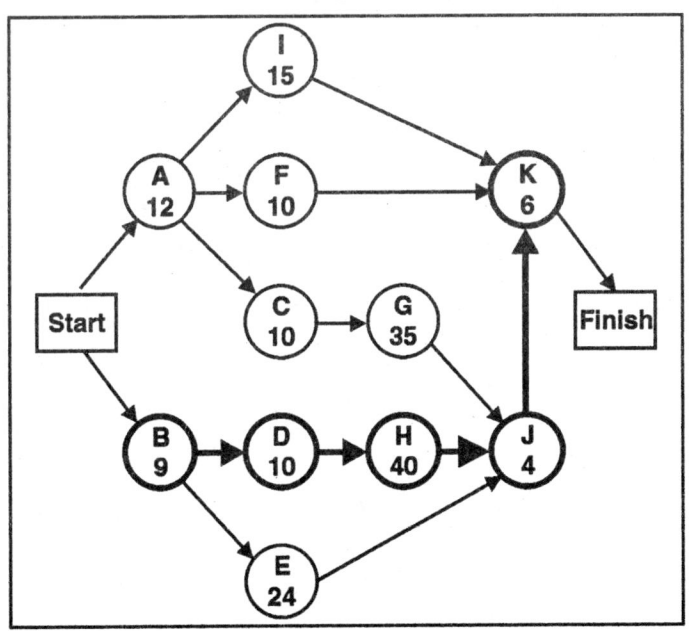

The expected time for the paths in the hospital project network are given in the following table.

Path	Expected time (wks)
A-I-K	33
A-F-K	28
A-C-G-J-K	67
B-D-H-J-K	69
B-E-J-K	43

The activity string B-D-H-J-K is expected to take the longest time (69 weeks) to complete. It is therefore the critical path for the hospital project and is shown in Figure 10.

As the critical path defines the completion time of the project, the focus should be on these activities in managing the project. These activities, which fall on the critical path, are called critical activities. However, projects can have more than one critical path. If activity A, C, or G were to fall behind by two weeks, the path A-C-G-J-K would be a second critical path. Consequently, managers should be aware that delays in activities not on the critical path could also cause delays in the entire project.

Manually finding the critical path in this way is easy for small projects; however, computers must be used for large, complex projects. Computers calculate activity slack and prepare periodic reports for managers to monitor progress. Activity slack is the maximum length of time that an activity can be delayed without delaying the entire project. Critical activities, i.e. activities on the critical path, have zero slack. Constantly monitoring the progress of activities with little or no slack enables managers to identify activities that need to be expedited to keep the project on schedule. Activity slack is calculated from four time units for each activity: i.e. earliest start time, earliest finish time, latest start time and latest finish time.

Earliest start and earliest finish times

The earliest start and earliest finish times are obtained by the following formula. The earliest finish time (EFT) of an activity equals its earliest start time plus its expected duration (t). This may be expressed as EFT = EST + t.

The earliest start time (EST) for an activity is the earliest finish time of the immediately preceding activity. For activities with more than one preceding activity, EST is the latest of the earliest finish time of the preceding activities.

To calculate the duration of the entire project, we determine the EFT for the last activity on the critical path.

Activity slack

Information on slack is useful to project managers because it helps them make decisions regarding reallocation of resources. Activities with zero slack are on the critical path. Resources could be taken from activities with slack and given to other activities that are behind schedule until the slack is used up. Activity slack can be calculated in one of the following two ways for any activity:

$$S = LST - EST \quad \text{or} \quad S = LFT - EFT$$

Figure 11: Network for the hospital project, showing data needed for activity slack calculation

Node	Duration in weeks	EST	LST	Slack
A	12	0	2	2
B	9	0	0	0
C	10	12	14	2
D	10	9	9	0
E	24	9	35	26
F	10	12	53	41
G	35	22	24	2
H	40	19	19	0
I	15	12	48	36
J	4	59	59	0
K	6	63	63	0

Calculating activity slack

Either starting times or finishing times can be used for calculation. Figure 12 shows the slack for each activity, using the formula LST − EST.

Figure 12: Calculation of activity slack

Node	Duration in weeks	EST	LST	Slack	
A	12	0	2	2	
B	9	0	0	0	←
C	10	12	14	2	
D	10	9	9	0	←
E	24	9	35	26	
F	10	12	53	41	
G	35	22	24	2	
H	40	19	19	0	←
I	15	12	48	36	
J	4	59	59	0	←
K	6	63	63	0	←

Activities B, D, H, J and K, marked with arrows, are on the critical path because they have zero slack.

The amount of slack for an activity depends on the performance of the activities leading to it. If the time for activity A had increased to 14 weeks instead of 12 weeks, the slack for activities C and G would be zero. Thus, slack is shared among all activities on a particular path.

Scheduling activities

The data in the PERT network gives information regarding the time at which a particular activity should be scheduled. This is usually done through the Gantt chart, which is a graphic format. It is very easy to understand and work with such a chart. A typical Gantt chart gives the following information at a glance:

- Project name
- Description of activities of the project
- Duration of the activity
- Scheduled starting date
- Scheduled finishing date
- Total float (slack) available for the activity
- Progress done to date (marked as V on the calendar)

The activities which are on the critical path are monitored more closely on the Gantt chart so that the milestones are achieved in the scheduled time. Gantt charts can be drawn and updated easily on the computer using project management software.

A typical Gantt chart is given in Figure 13.

Analysing resource requirement

A project would require different resources according to the activities to be completed. The core team of the project has to identify these resources for the

Figure 13: Gantt chart
(Progress recorded as on week 15)

S. No.	Activity Description	Duration (in weeks)	Calendar 1 2 3 4 5 6 7 8 9 10 11 12 13 14 15 16 17 18 19 20
A	Select staff	12	[▨▨▨▨▨▨▨▨▨▨▨▨]
B	Select site	9	[▨▨▨▨▨▨▨▨▨]◊
C	Select equipment	10	[▨▨▨▨]
D	Prepare construction plan	10	[▨▨▨▨▨▨▨]
E	Bring utilities to site	24	[▨▨▨▨▨▨▨▨▨▨▨▨▨◊]

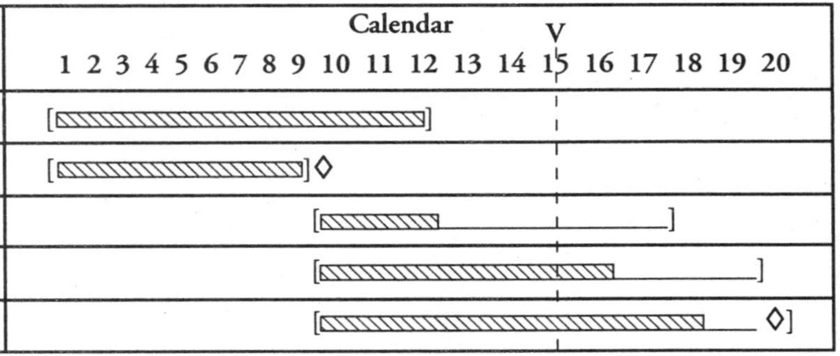

Legends

[Scheduled start
]   Scheduled finish
▨   Actual progress made
V   Current date (for progress report)
◊   Milestone scheduled

51

complete project. The resources may fall into the following categories:
- Manpower
- Money
- Equipment
- Facilities
- Materials and supplies
- Information
- Technology

The items which are available within the organisation also have to be identified. To make a budget for the project, the following is needed:
- The estimated cost of each resource: For the work force or labour, the hourly/daily or monthly rates have to be estimated. For other resources, it is better to get bids from the suppliers of materials, services and equipment.
- The availability of resources as per the requirements of the project: The timely availability should be checked from the suppliers.
- The estimated quality and output of manpower and equipment: This helps to choose the appropriate resources which are economical in the long run. If time is most important (e.g. for activities on the critical

path), then the fastest resource should be chosen. In case there is adequate time, then a resource that really saves money should be preferred.

Manpower requirement

The most important resource for a project is manpower. If people with the right background and experience are not available, then it would be very difficult to complete the project on time. For manpower planning, certain issues are important and must be kept in mind while selecting manpower.

- What are the skill sets required to complete a task?
- Where would the right manpower be available?
- How would the people working on the project be organised?

The manpower requirement should match the skills required in the tasks defined in the Work Breakdown Structure (WBS). For each task in the project, the following aspects have to be examined:

- Skill sets required for doing the task
- Type of experience required
- Additional skills required apart from technical skills, e.g. ability to communicate and negotiate
- Number of people required for each task at different levels

Skill requirement can be planned through the worksheet/template shown in Figure 14.

Figure 14: Worksheet for skill requirement for a project

| Project name: .... |
| Date: .... |
| Compiled by: .... |

S. No.	Tasks	Skill set required	Likely sources
1			
2			
3			
-			
-			

The skill sets available within the existing organisation also have to be examined before people are hired from outside sources.

A company which is engaged in many projects should maintain a network of suppliers and sources from which different services or inputs to the project can be procured. A list of sources and an inventory of skill sets available in the team can be useful for getting a replacement for any resource that is unavailable due to unforeseen circumstances. The skill sets are most important for the critical tasks of the project.

Estimates for supplies

For preparing a realistic budget, it is important to know the estimated cost. Whenever possible, it is desirable to get written estimates from suppliers of raw materials and capital equipment. The normal practice is to get competitive bids from different sources to have a more realistic budget. In case there is a separate purchase department in the organisation, it is better to use the template given in Figure 15 to specify the equipment and raw materials required.

Figure 15: Material and supplies worksheet

	Items required	Likely source or vendor	Quantity required	Date and time
Task:				
Date:				
Compiled by:				
a)	Material i) .... ii)			
b)	Supplies i) .... ii)			
c)	Capital equipment (machines, etc.) i) .... ii)			
d)	Special services i) .... ii)			

The materials and supplies should be procured from the potential sources identified in the figure. The items should be procured taking quality, price and time of delivery into account, in order to meet the requirements of the project.

Project budgeting and approval
Making a realistic budget is one of the most challenging tasks in project management. Budgeting skills improve with experience. The starting point for the budget is the work breakdown structure and its low level activities. Estimates have to be made for the cost of capital equipment and raw materials, labour cost and the indirect costs (rechargeable overheads). A typical worksheet for the preparation of a budget is given in Figure 16.

For budget preparation, the inputs regarding time estimates should be taken from the project team. In addition to that, the following sources should also be used:
- Suppliers of equipment and services: Their written estimates should be taken for budget preparation. For key items, samples may also be examined for their suitability for the project.
- Purchasing department staff: They may bring in their rich past experience of different

Figure 16: Budgeting worksheet

Project:		Date:		Prepared by:				
Task:		Dates:		Estimated costs:				
Number	Responsible person or vendor	Start	End	Equipment	Materials	Labour	Total	Actual

suppliers in terms of quality and delivery reliability.
- Certified experts: For highly specialised projects, it may be worthwhile to hire the services of an expert on the subject from within the organisation or from outside.

The rough budget is usually discussed with the sponsor before it is finally presented for approval.

Project Implementation

Project implementation means doing the tasks identified in the plan. Before implementation, it is important to check on the following tasks, which are prerequisite for effective implementation of the project plan:

- Key stages of the project identified
- Task list for initial key stages established
- Task durations estimated
- Task responsibility allocated and confirmed (for each key stage)
- Availability of resources confirmed
- Project milestones identified
- Gantt chart for each key stage finalised
- Reporting process established (status report format and frequency)
- Project meeting schedule prepared
- Project launch meeting preparations completed

Project launching

The project launch meeting is a milestone in a project. All the project work starts from then onwards. The purpose is to arrange a formal get-together of all the important persons involved in the project in order to explain the plans of the project. In the project launch meeting, the project manager usually invites:

- The project sponsor
- The customer
- Key stakeholders (within the organisation or external)
- The project team members

This is an important opportunity to explain the project, the areas of high risks and endorsement of the plan. The formal kick-off meeting may include a slide show or oral presentation by the project manager. In large/complex projects, it is worthwhile to give a folder to the participants which includes the following:

- Objectives of the project
- Project organisation chart
- Project stakeholders' list
- Key stage Gantt chart

- Key stage responsibility chart
- Project brief
- Any highlights of the project (e.g. use of new technology, etc.)

Project launching is usually done in a celebratory mood. It may be followed by a cultural programme to entertain the participants.

Organisational structure

For implementation of the project, the team may be organised in different ways. They include the following:

- Functional organisation
- Pure project organisation
- Matrix organisation

Functional organisation: This structure uses people from a functional department of the same organisation. Such an organisation is commonly established when a decision is taken at the executive level to initiate a project in the organisation. Almost all tasks are completed within one functional area, e.g. when a marketing campaign is launched by the marketing department of a company.

The functional organisation structure is diagrammatically represented in Figure 17.

Figure 17: A functional organisation structure

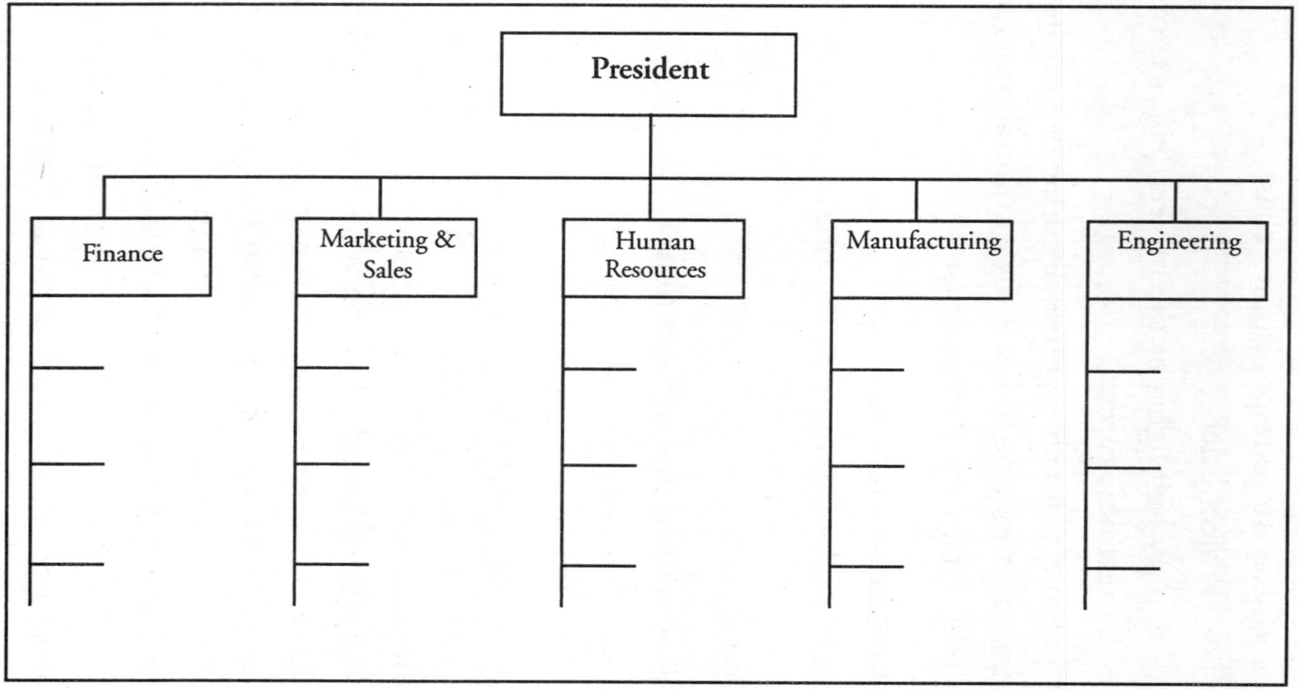

The advantages of the functional organisation structure are as follows:
- Familiarity of the members in terms of their skill and attitude
- Established administrative procedures which are already understood by the members
- Availability of staff for the project without any conflicts
- Efficient scheduling as the staff is present within the organisation
- Clear understanding of the line of authority and communication

The disadvantages of the functional organisation structure are limited resources, bureaucratic procedure and lack of project focus.

Pure project organisation: In such a structure, all the team members report to the project manager during the course of the project and members do not have any other responsibility. The pure project organisation structure is suitable for large projects or when the organisation business is project-oriented, e.g. a bridge construction company. This organisation structure is suitable when the duration of the project is a year or more.

The advantages of the pure project organisation structure are as follows:

- Clear line of authority due to unity of command
- Quick communication process and decision making
- Development of expertise among the team members in different components of the project work
- Clarity of focus among the members on the project and its priority

There are also certain limitations of pure project organisation:

- Possible duplication of effort if the company is running many projects at a time
- Attachment of team members to the project, as a result of which their assignment to other projects is resisted

The structure of a pure project organisation is given in Figure 18.

Matrix organisation: This structure uses functional supervisors as well as project supervisors to manage the same person, depending on the assignment. A strong matrix organisation almost works like a pure project organisation. The matrix organisation is

Figure 18: A pure project organisation structure

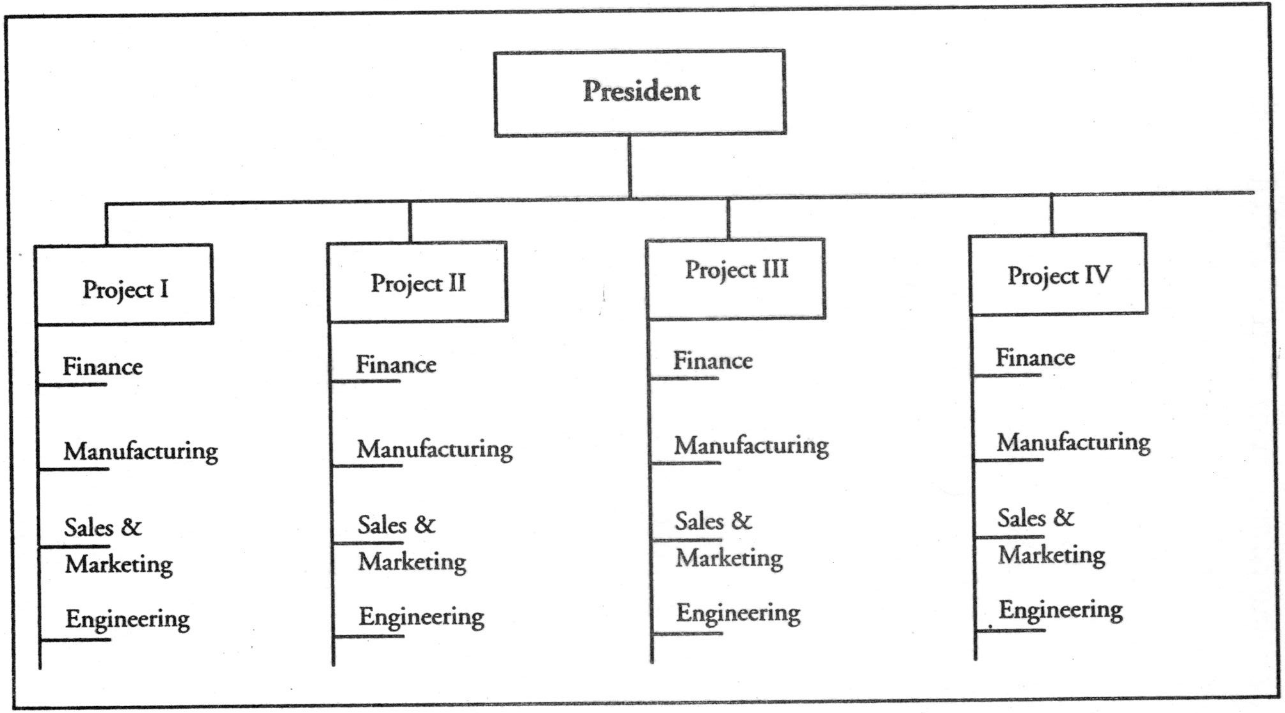

recommended when there is a need to share scarce resources in more than one project, e.g. a design or erection specialist may be assigned to multiple projects.

The matrix organisation structure has the following advantages:
- Clarity of focus on the task and its priority
- Highly flexible in order to make optimum use of the scarce resources of the organisation
- Allotment of new/challenging tasks possible, which leads to the development of skilled manpower
- Adaptive to changes in the business environment

The limitations of the matrix structure are as follows:
- More conflicts due to multiple authority and responsibilities
- After termination of a project, difficulty in integrating manpower into the mainstream
- Difficulty in the assessment of an employee's performance due to multiple bosses and responsibilities

A typical matrix organisation structure, where people are allotted to different departments for specific projects, is shown in Figure 19.

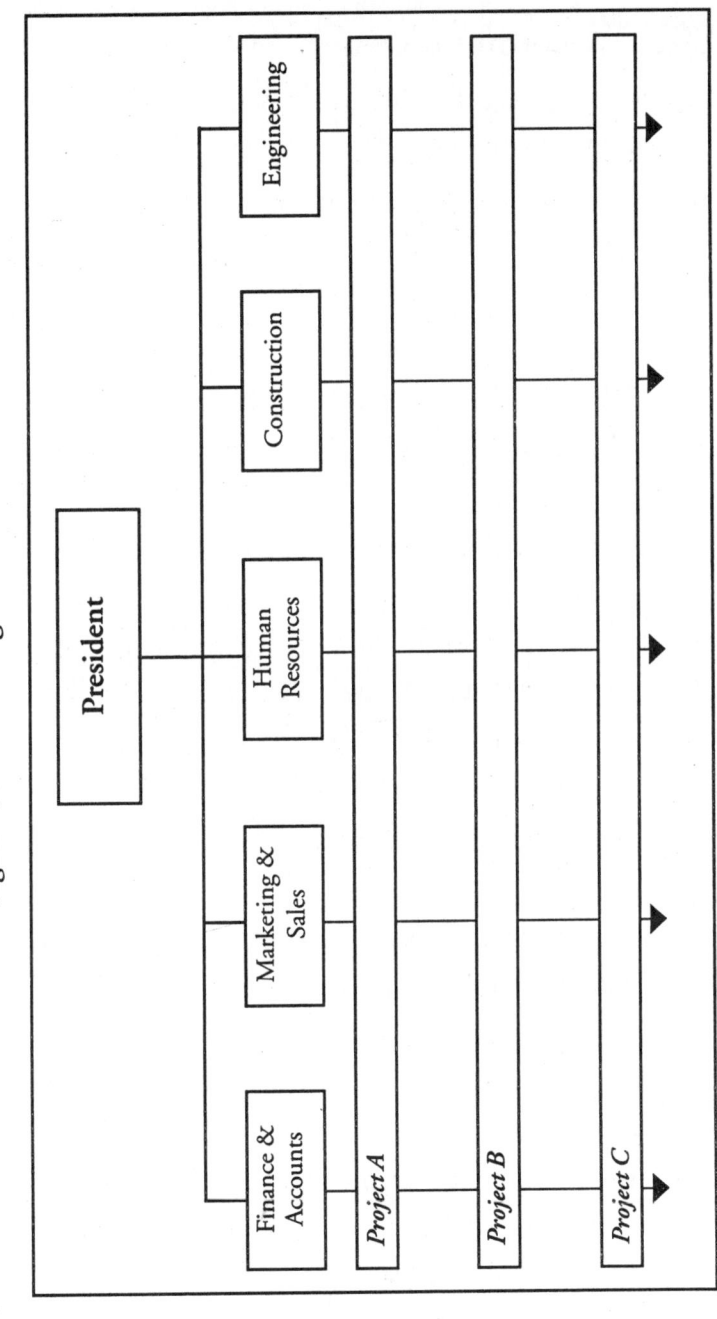
Figure 19: A matrix organisation structure

Effective communication

Effective communication is very important for implementation of the project. Poor communication is a major source of conflict and slippage and can cause unnecessary delays.

The issues in communication are as follows:
- Who needs to know
- What is the information they need to know
- How much of the information they need to know
- How often they need to know

The information communicated should be useful. There is no point in sending large volumes of information which will never be read by the recipient. Communication is important in the following directions:
- Upward communication (for sponsors and key stakeholders)
- Horizontal communication (for other project leaders, suppliers, etc.)
- Downward communication (for the project team – this has to be detailed enough to do the work)
- Incoming communication (for listening to the concerns, difficulties and risks involved or problems anticipated)

Channels of communication

In project management, a large amount of communication is carried out through written reports, but in today's environment, there are a number of alternative channels for communication. The advantages and limitations of different channels are listed for optimal choice of channels of communication.

Electronic media
- Telephone calls and voice mail
    - good for personal, short communication
    - can reach remote locations
    - non-availability of the person at the other end is a limitation
    - may not be suitable for prolonged discussions
- Email and fax
    - very quick and precise, like a written report
    - lacks privacy, and the biggest limitation is that it may not be read by the recipient

Written communication
- Handwritten short notes
    - quick and friendly way to communicate with a person who is nearby

- ideal for conveying appreciation of work and thanks
- Formal written reports
  - ideal for reporting about progress and important procedures for which a permanent record is essential
  - needs clarity so that the receiver can understand it
  - long reports may not be read fully

Face-to-face communication
- Formal meetings
  - ideal when communication has to be with multiple persons and there is a need to get feedback/confirmation of the message
  - large number of issues can be discussed in one meeting
  - meetings may be a waste of time for many people, especially if they are only marginally concerned with the issues under discussion
  - some people may feel uncomfortable expressing a dissenting note in a public meeting
- Formal presentations
  - ideal for presenting complex issues/ procedures which need understanding

- audiovisual presentations are easy to understand and leave a positive impression
- calls for skill and preparation to make a good presentation, so it is not suitable for all people
- poor presentation can negatively affect the project

In addition to the above channels, 'management by walking around' is an informal method of communication for the project manager. It essentially means visiting the project site personally, walking around and chatting with team members. This technique has the following advantages:

- builds morale and rapport with the project team
- improves the quality and timeliness of the project
- gives a realistic assessment of the progress made
- gives an insight into the problems and working environment of the team members
- makes it possible to refocus certain issues or solve problems promptly
- builds visibility of the project leader and emphasises his/her approachability

Project status reports

Project status reports are the most important reports to be sent to the project sponsors and the key stakeholders on a regular basis. Such reports are based on the inputs received from the key team members. It is preferable to have a standard template for the regular progress reports so that key points are not missed in a report.

Project status reports highlight the progress made in respect of the milestones fixed earlier in the planning stage. The major components of a status report are as follows:

- Summary of the overall progress made
- List of milestones due to be completed since the previous report and the current status of progress made
- List of milestones due in the next report
- Actions taken to rectify any slippages stated in the earlier report
- Forecast for the completion of the project, based on the current status
- Reasons for any changes in forecasts made in the past
- Report of any risk which has become an issue and needs resolution

It is up to the project manager to decide the frequency of the different reports for small and large projects.

Project implementation meetings

Meetings are an important part of project management, for briefing as well as debriefing on the progress of the project. The project manager must decide on the essential meetings for the smooth execution of the project process. These include the following:

- One-to-one meetings with project sponsors
- One-to-one meetings with team members
- Project progress meetings with team members
- Problem-solving meetings
- Meetings with key stakeholders

One-to-one meetings are extremely important to build rapport with the sponsors and the team members of a project. The frequency of the meetings should be decided with due consultation and then put into the meeting schedule and Gantt chart. Problem-solving meetings are usually ad hoc in nature and such meetings are organised at short notice. Short meetings are usually held at the end of the week.

Management of project problems

Problems are inherent in any project in spite of the best of planning. The problems may arise due to various factors, including the following:

- The tasks may take longer than the estimated time
- Adequate manpower may not have been assigned to the job
- Resources like money, people, equipment and materials may not be available when required
- Technical difficulties may arise with existing or new technologies
- Adequate skills may not be available amongst team members
- Monitoring may not be adequate
- Conflicts and misunderstanding may have taken place within the team or with external stakeholders

A potential risk becomes an issue when it takes the form of a problem. Before trying to solve the problem, the first step is to understand the problem. The project team has to state the perceived problem. The second step is to identify the cause of the problem. There are two specialised techniques that may be used for identifying the cause of the problem:

- Fish bone diagram (also known as Ishikawa diagram)
- Pareto analysis

The fish bone diagram (Figure 20) is developed by examination of all the possible causes under four standard headings.

- People
- Process/method
- Materials
- Equipment

Figure 20: Fish bone diagram

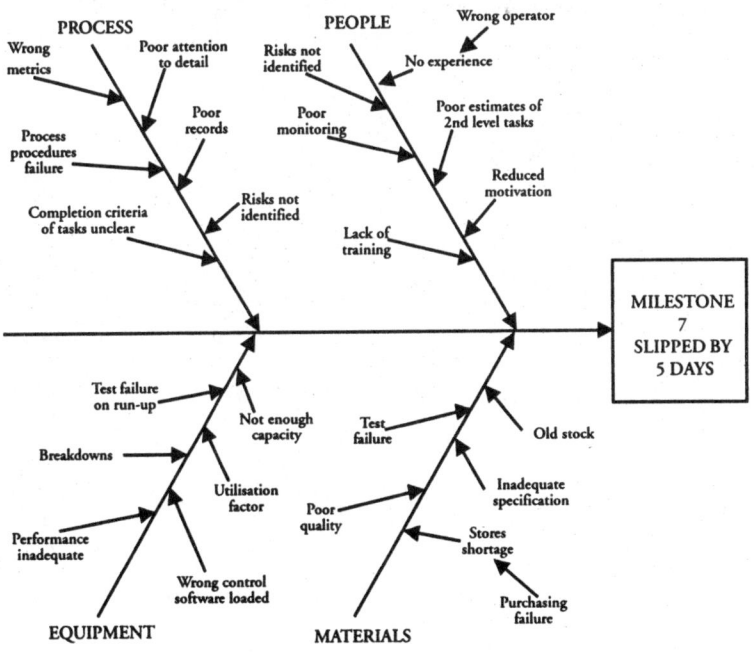

The problem is written in the square box on the right-hand side and five lines are drawn as shown in Figure 20. The problem illustrated here indicates that a particular milestone (No 7) has slipped by five days. The possible causes are listed under the appropriate headings as shown in the diagram. The secondary causes can also be identified in the diagram.

There are rarely any readymade solutions to all problems and alternative solutions have to be developed through brainstorming sessions. The basic rules for brainstorming are as follows:

- All members are equal (i.e. no hierarchy)
- One member may act as a moderator/recorder
- All members understand the problem and its scope
- Members think over the problem and offer solutions one at a time
- Each suggestion is noted by the moderator *without any discussion* or value judgement at this stage (even if the suggestion is impractical, crazy or stupid)
- All the alternative suggestions received for the implementation of the suggestions in the first round are listed in the second round

- The advantages and limitations of each suggestion are discussed and the possible solutions/actions for implementation are identified

In the brainstorming session where members build on the suggestions of other members, a particular suggestion does not remain the monopoly of one person but it becomes the outcome of the group's effort. This helps in implementation of the solutions developed through the brainstorming technique.

Pareto analysis is another powerful tool to identify key problems. There may be many factors responsible for creating a problem. Pareto analysis isolates the important few factors (types of defects) from many other unimportant ones. The factors and their corresponding frequency are plotted on a graph like a bar chart. The chart has two vertical axes, the left-hand one showing frequency as in a histogram and the right-hand vertical axis showing the cumulative percentage of frequency. The cumulative frequency curve identifies the few vital factors that need the attention of the management. A typical Pareto chart for different defect types is shown in Figure 21. It shows that defects C and D account for more than 80% of the problem and therefore need attention first.

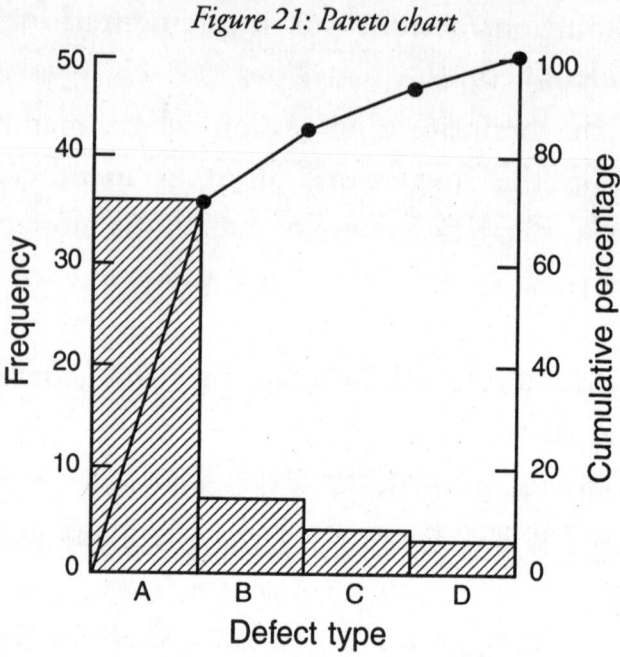

Figure 21: Pareto chart

Project logbook

The purpose of a project logbook is to record all events related to the project. It is usually a bound, lined book, kept by the project manager. The logbook is *not* a personal document, but an addendum to the project file. The entries in the logbook are done by the project manager. They include all records of agreed actions and forward-planning ideas. The records are kept date-wise and each day starts on a new page. Records include key

points and references to the concerned events/ persons. The typical events recorded include the following:
- Memos, letters, faxes, telephone calls sent and received
- Purchase instructions issued
- Contracts signed
- Action plans agreed upon
- Problems encountered and solutions derived
- Important decisions taken and how they were implemented
- Reports issued
- Meetings held and decisions taken

The entries are made in ink and not with pencil. The pages are numbered and are not supposed to be torn or removed from the book. The logbook is an invaluable record for ready reference by the project manager. It also helps in post-project evaluation. It is an important document for resolution of conflicts and disputes.

Project monitoring

Monitoring the time and cost variance during the implementation of the project is an important function of project management. Monitoring is

usually done by graphically plotting the following three costs against the time schedule of the project:
- Actual cost of the work completed on date
- Budgeted cost of the work completed on date
- Budgeted cost of the work scheduled

Figure 22 clearly shows the cost overrun and also the amount of time by which the project is running behind schedule.

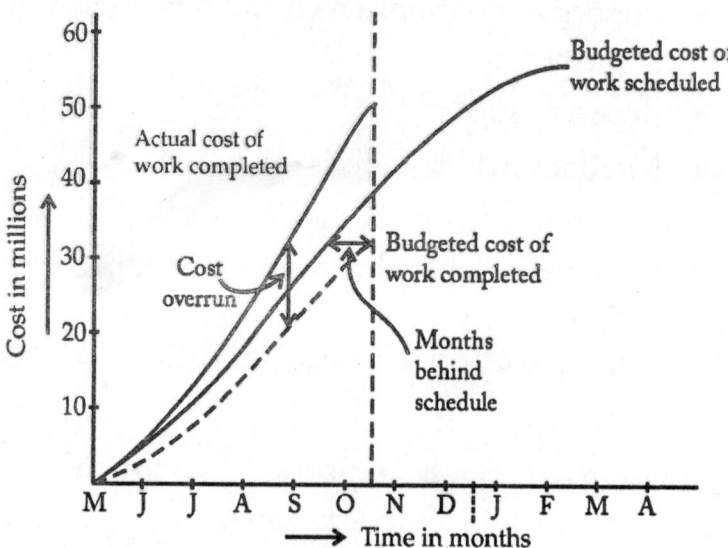

Figure 22: Project cost control diagram

Application of computers

In typical projects the number of activities is very large and it becomes difficult to apply PERT manually. Hence, computers are used for this purpose. There are many types of software available

for project management. The input data required include the following:
- List of activities to complete the project
- Estimates for the duration of the activities
- Precedence requirements for individual activities, i.e. which activities must be completed before the activity under reference can start

The software can generate the PERT network, identify the critical path, draw a Gantt chart for scheduling of activities and schedule the activities on a calendar.

Project Handover Phase

Every project has to reach a logical conclusion. In the closing phase of a project, many activities have to be carried out. The project has to be checked for its completion before it is formally handed over to the customer. The closure should have the approval of the key stakeholders also. Projects provide an opportunity to learn and hence they need to be documented for future use.

Concluding tasks

The major tasks in the closure stage are as follows:

Approval of the stakeholder: The project is launched on account of the stakeholders and therefore their formal approval for completion is also important. This may be done informally in small projects but in large projects, the report on the project is also approved formally.

Contractual commitments: The project takes help/inputs from a large number of suppliers of various resources like raw materials, equipment and technical services. The accounts of these people have to be settled. Sometimes letters of thanks or appreciation may also be issued for jobs well done.

Project handover: The project has to satisfy the quality/specifications agreed upon at the beginning. The obligatory performance test may also have to be conducted in the case of manufacturing projects. In the case of infrastructure projects like a plant, the operation has to be carried out by the customer. For this purpose there are reports, drawings and operating instructions which have to be handed over to the customer.

Redeployment of manpower: A project is a one-time activity and therefore the team members have to go back to their parent departments after the conclusion of the project. Sometimes performance evaluation also has to be completed before they are deployed in another project.

Release of resources: At the end of a project, raw materials, consumables and equipment should be disposed of suitably. The waste materials also have to be removed to clean the project site.

Completion of accounts: The accounts for payables and receivables, if any, are completed for the project in this phase.

Project documentation: Each project is a learning experience and in large projects, a final report is prepared.

Termination procedure

The steps involved in the termination of a project are as follows:

Decision to terminate: The project manager should do an inspection to check that the tasks have been completed and the final touches have been given to make the project ready for handover to the customer.

Documentation for handover: This has to be completed as planned. It should also include the small tasks which are required for the finishing touch.

Concluding meeting: The project manager should organise a meeting with all the team members to acknowledge their contribution to the project. In successful projects, this is usually an event for celebration.

Communication: Written communication to all the concerned people is important before formal conclusion of the project so that pending bills are settled before its final termination.

A large project checklist is prepared for the project winding-up process. A typical checklist for this purpose is given in Figure 23.

Figure 23: Checklist for termination of a project

Activity Description	Required	Responsible		Remarks regarding target date, etc.
		Yes	No	
Identify remaining tasks Dispose materials Redeploy/store equipment Close out work orders Plan termination Settle accounts with vendors Notify purchasing department Audit final changes Evaluate personnel Reassign staff Hand over engineering/ operational documents Final delivery instructions Concluding staff meeting Final report of project Concluding review meeting				

The final report on a project is a document which gives the history and implementation of the project in brief. Most of the information could come from the project logbook maintained by the project manager.

The important contents of the final project report are as follows:
- Overview of the project plan
- Achievement of the project goals
- Financial accounting of the project
- Evaluation of performance in terms of quality and delivery
- Evaluation of team performance
- Risks in the project and their management
- Technical or managerial learnings from the project
- Acknowledgement of the contribution of team members and key stakeholders.

Glossary

activity   a clearly defined task or tasks with known duration; usually a group of tasks which together complete a particular step or part of the work

activity-on-node diagram   a network diagram where all activities are represented by the node or event, usually as a box, and the arrows are used merely to show the logical flow of the project

backward pass   the procedure by which the latest event times or the finish and start times for the activities of a network are determined

bar chart   a graphical presentation of the activities of a project derived from the project logic diagram shown as a timed schedule

budgeted cost of work scheduled	the final 'frozen' plans signed off by the sponsor before implementation. This is also called the recorded or baseline plan, against which all progress is measured and variances analysed and reported
budgeted cost of work completed	the budgeted cost, based on the operating budget, of the work that is actually completed up to a particular point in the project schedule
close out work orders	the process by which a work order is completed by tying up any loose ends
control system	the procedures established at the start of the project to provide the leader with the necessary data to compare the planned status with the actual status at any instant in time, in order to identify variances and to take corrective action

cost control diagram — a graphical representation of the actual and budgeted costs of the work actually performed against the scheduled and budgeted costs of the work planned

cost variance — the difference between the value of the work actually performed and the actual costs incurred and committed

critical activity — an activity in the project (falling on the critical path) that has been analysed to show it has zero float and must therefore be completed on time if the project is not to slip

critical path — the sequence of activities which determines the total time for the project

deliverable — a specific, defined, measurable and tangible output from the project. Most projects have several deliverables

dependency   the basic rule of logic governing project logic diagrams and network drawing: any activity which is dependent on another is normally shown to emerge from the head event of the activity on which it depends

duration   the estimated or actual time required to complete an activity

EFT   the earliest finish time of an activity without changing total time or the spare or float time

EST   the earliest start time of an activity

event   a point in the progress of the project after total completion of all the preceding activities

float   the difference between the time necessary and the time available for an activity

Gantt chart	A graphical method of depicting a project schedule which shows project time, date, all activities, resources and their relationships. It is derived from the project logic diagram when it has been analysed for float
issue	a risk to the project, or an unforeseen event that has become a reality and needs to be resolved if the project integrity is not to be threatened
key stages	a group of closely related activities that can be isolated together as a clear stage of the project, and which must be completed before passing to the next stage
lag	an intentional delay period of time introduced between two activities in a project logic diagram
LFT	the latest possible finish time without changing the total task or float times

LRC	the linear responsibility chart that displays a complete listing of key stages and/or activities with the names of the resource person(s) who have been allocated responsibility for each activity as part of the plan
LST	the latest possible time an activity can start without affecting the total project time
milestone	another name for an event, but usually reserved for a significant or major event in the project. It is often used for identifying key progress reporting points
monitoring	the process of checking what is happening and collecting data on project progress
PERT diagram	the project logic diagram in the PERT (Programme Evaluation Review Technique) project control system
predecessor	the activity immediately prior to an event

project approved budget   the budget approved at the conception of the project, based on outline plans, only with contingency included

project file   a central file that must contain copies of all documentation, letters, faxes, etc. relating to the project. It is the project archive and the basis for subsequent evaluation and continuous improvement in activities

project lifecycle   a systems approach to a project where the project is described as passing through four phases, from conception to termination

project logbook   a bound A4 book with numbered pages in which the project leader records all events, action plans and project activities. It comprises a complete event record cross-referenced to the project file. On larger projects, each team member should maintain a project logbook

project logic diagram	a graphic representation of the activities in a project with clearly identified logical dependencies established
project steering team	a senior management committee often made up of project sponsors who have the power to prioritise and steer projects in the direction necessary to meet corporate objectives
resource	anything, other than time, which is needed for carrying out an activity. It is most commonly restricted to people involved in the project
risk	an event that has been identified as potentially threatening to the project's integrity if it actually happens
risk log	a sequential listing of all risks identified throughout the project life, and information about their ranking, probability and management

schedule	the project plan converted to 'real time' against a calendar by inserting realistic agreed time estimates and resource capacity factors into all the project activities
schedule variance	the difference between the value of the work completed and the budgeted cost, from the operating budget, of the work planned to be completed at a particular point in the schedule
soft project	a project where the objectives are only broadly stated and the resources needed are unknown and flexible, the scope left open intentionally and deadlines not defined clearly
sponsor	the senior manager who takes ownership of the project on behalf of the organisation
stakeholder	any individual who has an interest or stake in the project at any time during the project lifecycle. The interest may be positive or negative

successor	the activity immediately following an event
task	a specific defined piece of work usually carried out by one person in a finite measurable period of time; a sub-unit of a project activity
total float	the total spare time possessed by an activity beyond the estimated duration
work breakdown structure (WBS)	the diagrammatic representation of all the key stages and their associated activities arranged in a hierarchical format, showing each level of planning
work plan	a standard format form or chart for recording an agreed listing of the tasks to be carried out by an individual or department, complete with agreed start and finish times for each within the overall project schedule